# Lord Shiva

## The 'Intense' Lover.

(Not A Fiction)

Richa Srivastava



BlueRose ONE.com
Stories Matter
NewDelhi • London

**BLUEROSE PUBLISHERS**
India | U.K.



For permissions requests or inquiries regarding this publication, please contact:

BLUEROSE PUBLISHERS
www.BlueRoseONE.com
info@bluerosepublishers.com
+91 8882 898 898
+4407342408967

ISBN: 978-93-6783-131-1

Cover Design: Aman Sharma
Typesetting: Pooja Sharma

First Edition: December 2024

# *Dedication*

I dedicate this book to my father late Mr. Swatantra Kumar and my Mother Mrs. Krishna Srivastava.

# About the Author

Richa Srivastava is well known for her professionalism and achievements. Having a vast background of IP, she already had 2 startups in the past related to IP and Content. She has been a beauty pageant finalist for the year 2019 and went Greece for finale. She is an Author, counselor, motivational speaker. Already published an E-book on Kindle, she believes in learning new things to mark her presence with confidence. She has been awarded with a government honor of BrandIndia: women in business award 2021, Indian Achievers Award 2021, Foxclues india's top 100 women icon 2021 and Glantor X women in leadership award 2022. She is also awarded with the Desh Ratan Award for writer in 2024, Rabindra Ratan Puraskar 2024 for Writer, identified as Top 100 outstanding women for 2024 from Diva planet Magazine, her presence published in LIFESTYLE MAGAZINE, received " International Achievers Award 2024" from Height of Success Magazine and Last but not the least she received WORLD RECORD FOR HER EXCEPTIONAL SKILL IN MOTIVATIONAL SPEAKING AND WRITING in June 2024. Also, a verified writer of yourquote. One can find her LinkedIn profile on top when she is searched by her name on google.

# About The Book

This book is a symbol of true love and devotion for Lord Shiva and how Shiva reciprocates the love by showing his presence in this physical world. You will get a chance to read real-life experiences of Lord Shiva in my life and how it impacted my life and wisdom. I never read any mythological book or scriptures to gain knowledge of Shiva or any other God Goddess of that matter but my connection with Shiva helps me to understand the world through my own wisdom and thoughts. This book is my journey to understand and reach Shiva through my own wisdom.

As per my understanding Lord Shiva is a pure energy of love. As the story unfold you will find various incidents where you can relate to evil as well as God which is enough to compel you to believe in God and shake you up for devotion.

You need to be a pure soul if you want to be loved by Shiva and get protected. By the end of this book, you will understand how intense he could love someone if you love him intensely.

# Contents

# 1. My Arrival

Arrival "*to aise likha hai jaise main koi Avtar hoon*". Anyway, let's start the story.

I belong to a middleclass family which turn out to be upper middle with time. At the era of my young mom and papa they both were "*pujari*" kind of. My maternal grandmother was the big one. My mom used to enjoy these rituals which my *nani* which she follows every day and my mother has the responsibilities to keep everything ready before *pooja*. My mom was the one to clean cloths and utensils of God and Goddess of her temple at home.

My mom always tells us an incident which gave me goosebumps when I heard it for the first time. She told me that one fine day she was washing *lota* for the pooja with full devotion for MAA DURGA and when she washed it completely, she found a mettle sheet inside that lota with MAA DURGA engraved on it. I was shocked to hear this, how is this possible? But my mom said it was because of devotion and there was a vibe of party that day in my maternal house whole day.

My mom belongs to the time when marriages used to be fixed by parents and husband wife don't see each other. My *nana* was impressed by papa as he was an engineer and having vast knowledge of Hindi and Sanskrit. I remember papa used to recite all *shlokas* of *Geeta* in Sanskrit.

As my mom explains, papa and whole clan of him came to see mom and she was also trying to see papa but she couldn't. I think she is shy to say "*beta sabko nahi dekh sakte the tab*" 😊 So, the marriage happened and after one year I was inside my mom to come in this world with lots of mysteries, experiences and love. Mummy told me that she started bleeding during pregnancy as she pushed something very hard though I survived *kyuki mujhe to ana hi tha duniya dekhne.*

The month of May was destined for my arrival. It was 11th May evening, when my mother undergone surgery to bring me out. And to everyone surprise ice cubes started falling in the extreme hot month of summer with rain and thunderstorms. Everyone enjoyed, but that was first time when they witnessed such sudden weather change in May. I arrived, when my mom came in senses papa said to mummy "*beti ko dekhe hain ji kitni sundar hai*" and my mom again became unconscious.

# 2. Childhood Incidents

I was fond of Banana in Childhood. I don't know how because what I realized now, I hate banana.

I was 3 years old when my family along with *Chacha*, *Bua* went to Market in Malda (it's a place in West Bengal) where my father was posted as engineer in NHPC (National Hydroelectric Power Corporation). Everyone was getting down from Jeep one by one no one was bothering where I am sitting as my *chacha* was holding me. Soon the bomb blasted as no one was able to see me around. My mom started crying and whole clan distributed in market to search me. No one was able to find me. My mother says when she confirmed herself that she has lost me forever I myself came back to her out of nowhere and when she asked me how I managed I didn't have an answer. Market was damn crowded all I remember; I was holding some lady's finger who was in very dark red lipstick and big red bindi and said "*main tumhari mummy nahi hoon*". I don't know how I searched my mother in *Chandani chowk* kind of market but that reminds me of miracle that Shiva was with me to protect me that time.

In Second incident my mom gave me bath and send me out with our servant named *Fulena* I used to call him

*Funna* 😊. I was in his lap but he put me down at a place where some goods were getting loaded as someone got transferred from Malda. He was unaware that septic main hole was open and I fell in to it. Without knowing the repercussion of this incident, he started helping in loading goods with a thought that he may get some money. But now it was getting late and my mom came out to search me. It was not the era of mobile phone so people used to walk more for work and concerns. She reached him and asked where am I and he was stunned as I was not standing beside him. Mummy slapped him and thought that I might have fell inside septic tank. Mummy kicked him inside the septic tank to search me, and he said yes, I was there sitting and crying. He pushed me up and I was stinking like hell. My mom gives this credit of escape to MAA DURGA to give this sense where I could be. I remember I took bath trice to be me.

My parents always see *mahurat* before going out for a journey by road but what if you have to travel through train? Well, you can't see *mahurat* and misfortune could happen any time. Train was already started and my papa put me on the gate of a boggy but it was getting faster so all other members get inside another boggy. All were scared as I was only 3 someone just closed the door so that I be safe but I had no idea where to go, fortunately one driver uncle was there from NHPC who hold me till my parents came to take me on next station.

# 3. Schooling, Roaming and College Love

My father was in Central Government job so there was a transfer in every 4-5 years across India. My initial schooling was in DAV and more in *Kendriya Vidyalaya* as it's a government school present inside every government residential society of NHPC. My first school was DAV *Khunti* though, and I remember I was in class 2nd when I saw the first blue eyed beautiful boy who was younger to me in school premises. He was starring me when I was playing and I was little uncomfortable. I saw him few days doing same. One day he was following me when I was alone and I was thinking "*ye baccha mere peeche kyun pada hai?*" And he was saying "*a ruko mujhe baat karni hai*" though I didn't listen to him. He said to his friend "*ye mujhse baat kyun nahi karti?*" One day while returning back to home I was sitting in Bus when my friend said "*dekh wo tujhe bula raha hai*" I didn't respond as I was shy. when he went, I asked "*blue eyes wala?*" she said "*nahi uski eyes to brown hai*", I was not scared as his eyes were blue only, I was sure, I thought my friend got confuse.

We used to play some stone game in soil in childhood which I don't remember exactly. That day my friend went to wash room and out of nowhere that blue eyed boy appeared in front of my eye he looked in my eye and said "**darna mat, main aunga, main shaadi karunga tumse, wait karna, tum meri ho**" and he vanished. Again, I was not scared but my inner voice said "*tumhari doosri saadi hogi*". I got engaged in my childish thoughts "*main to mummy papa ki hoon iski kaise ho gai? Aur shaadi to ek baar hi hoti hai*". That was the last time I saw that blue eyed beautiful boy in my entire schooling of DAV. He was not seen to anyone and my friend didn't remember anything. That was my first encounter with GOD SHIVA.

I was very bad in studies initially, my mathematics had to start with 0 and end on 0. I remember papa used to throw my math book while he teaches me. Maximum slaps I have received is because of math. In $10^{th}$ board exam I remember I was sure of failing but I think I passed only due to my prayers. I just got passing marks 35 and a total percentage of second class. To be honest I thought now math will never appear in my life ever but it is a subject which can never leave you. It is so much involved in daily life and practices that it is a kind of ritual you can't get rid of.

After $10^{th}$ I chose Biology and went to Nainital boarding for $11^{th}$ class. It was the first time I was away from home and learning to survive without parents. I was naive in so many things and learning how people treat and behave with other in different situations and scenarios. We used to go to city outings on Sundays and I remember Hindi medium girls used to put more makeup on face while going out 😊. Mine was a girl's school so Sunday was the only day we were allowed to see boys 😊. We went out one day and one parents with his extremely good-looking son came to talk to us to get feedback about boy's schools in Nainital. I saw the color of their son eyes, which were quite impressive though parents had normal eyes. As they went, I said to my classmates "*aankh ka colour kitna acha tha*" and they were "*kya acha tha black hi to tha*". I just thought "*kya bakwas hai*" though I didn't discuss more. I was surrounded with unique kind of people in my childhood. There was a girl in 11$^{th}$ who told to everyone herself after admission that no one should befriend with her else that girl will fail and she will pass. It was happening with her since childhood but who would have believed such stupid thing. One girl beceme a very good friend of her and at the end same happened as she announced earlier, that girl failed she passed. There are so many strange things in this world but people don't believe unless they experience it, I have witnessed it.

Now, again it was the Time my father got promoted and transferred to Indore (Madhya Pradesh), a beautiful city of India also known as mini-Mumbai. Here, I got admission in class 12$^{th}$ and again got a chance to stay with my family. I was kind of introvert even with girls but I believe I was beautiful that's the reason girls were little jealous. I remember they played some conspiracy with few guys of commerce department about which boys were unknown and later on every one said sorry to me for their deed. There was a girl in my class, I never liked, Simi. One morning she came to me and said "*I saw a dream and your husband's name is Rishi Sinha*". she said my dreams generally comes true. I was naïve, though it was weird still my heart wanted to believe it. But now I have met few people whose dream symbolize future truth. It was school annual day and I had some work so I came back in class, song was playing in background "*jisse dhoodhta to main har kahin, jo kahin mili mujhe hai nahi*" and someone crossed my class. I only noticed the height and physic, which was quite impressive. I wanted to see him again but when I asked about him to my classmate who were present there but, no one had seen him. This time eye color was black but he was very attractive and as usual again he vanished. The beauty of these incidents are I never gave importance to it and never got involved. I never had a best friend too because of papa's transferable job so, never get a chance to come too close to anyone. Still, I miss that connection, some bonds are to be built at childhood only.

Due to some conspiracy this time papa was transferred to Lucknow after spending one year only at Indore.

Lucknow was not new to us. We had visited there quite a few times when we were staying in Tanakpur NHPC project. Lucknow is capital of Uttar Pradesh one of the most popular states of North India and known of its old Heritage and Chikankari work on cloths. It was a turning point of my life as I had to make decision of my future career after achieving 60% somehow in class 12$^{th}$. My parents wanted me to become doctor and after failing all the medical entrance exam directly after 12$^{th}$ they want me to do coaching for a year to get into medical. But one article changed my perspective towards career. There was an article on Biotechnology and it was explained there in very impressive way that why one should make a career in it. Its future and salary aspects too. It was very impressive and inviting for me. It completely changed my mind and I decided to do biotechnology next year. There were very few colleges in India that time who were offering curriculum in Biotechnology, one of them was JNU. I shifted from Medical to Biotech and I don't regrate it after seeing medical curriculum. (with all due respect to doctors).

Internet was quite new that time and so the online chat. I was using sify.com in which a window called lovers lane was there where I got an "HI" from "Rishi". As whole world I was also excited to know ASL on chat box when someone new used to ping me. As per ASL he was Rishi

Sinha, Male, Varanasi but native of Lucknow. I got goosebumps. It recalled me of simi's prophecy. I was shocked (just feel how idiot I was). Rishi Sinha could be anyone but I had already started dreaming of my life partner. (now, I feel why people say don't marry before 30). He was a good looking guy doing B.Tech from IT BHU and was a student of second year. We used to talk as friend initially and then the time came when result came out and as it usually happens, I failed JNU so, my parents decided to send me Bangalore to study Biotechnology in one of the oldest institutes there known as "MS Ramaiah College of Art, Science, and Commerce".

I didn't opt for college hostel and preferred to stay out in a private hostel which was more hygienic and disciplined than campus hostel. Though again, now I feel I should have opted for campus only I might had made good friends. Anyway, first day of college, excitement was high and was dreaming of good friends, parties, bonding, freedom, and of course to become a good student study wise too. My roommate was not good she used to steal a lot of money from me and I shifted her to another room after 2 years. She was very nice to me so it took some time to uncover her real face.

College life was good but I restricted myself from so many things I believe. I was a very obedient daughter so missed all the fun. We were a group of 7 in college 5 boys 2 girls including me. We had great bonding; people were jealous of our friendship and dedication for each other. But it remained only for one year, friends started getting more friends and everything shattered. Guys used to like me but as the prophecy of Simi I already considered Rishi to be my future husband.

He used to talk very rarely; he didn't had phone that time. After completing his B.Tech he chose to come to Bangalore Branch of his company as I was here. I don't even remember who proposed first but, things was moving as per simi's dream. I remember one day I was talking to Rishi over mobile phone when he was in Bangalore and my intercom rang and I heard a guy crying "*Richa, I see you every day when u go to college,*" I asked his name he replied "*Venkatesha*" I said "*I don't know you*", he said "*don't say like that I know you from ages*" I laughed and hang the call. He never called again.

I was in second year when I got a back in Chemistry, it was quite shocking for me as I really did well in all the papers and I was actually improving in studies with time. Lecturer announced that back paper students will have to give re-examination. I was not ready for it and couldn't accept it. Though I sensed a kind of conspiracy still I decided to see my fate so I thought not to give exam and see how much I get after rechecking. Papa didn't say anything he knew I was improving. When the result came, I passed, I knew it. My mates were shocked and asked "*how come you were so sure*"? I said "*I know what I had done in examination*" they said "*still you know the Universities right, lot of things happens*", I said "*My believe in God was unshakeable, I was getting strength from there only*".

One of my juniors from Nainital also joined Ramaiah in different department. I saw her first time on the way to college, she was also excited to see me. She informed me that now our warden is dead. I was little upset; she was a nice lady. I remember, I again saw her in Auditorium she ran to me " *Richa di aap yahan, kab se?*" I was shocked and said "*abhi to bahar mile the*", she said "*main to apse pehli baar mil rahi hoon yahan*" As usual It didn't bother me more.

One day I saw my roommate going back to hostel, she was ahead of me (that time we were in same room) to reach her fast I crossed the road without seeing that a bike was coming to me in full speed. He hit me so hard that I jumped in sky and fallen down, though I stand up so biker got scared and ran away. People came to me so my roommate too. I had little difficulty in walking though. Those who saw the accident were saying "*ye bach kaise gai?*". That time my mom was sitting on *pooja* and she got a view of me in blood, hurriedly she said my sister to call me if I am fine. My roommate informed that I met an accident but "*she is fine*". In the hospital she made me sit at a place and a doctor came. Doctor was very handsome and eye colour was very different. I lied down on stretcher and he touched my feet and was smiling and moved it in one direction and said "*bas ho gaya , She is all fine now*". He went. As I moved out of the room, I saw my roommate again coming with a doctor. She said "*doctor ko dikha do*" I said "*abhi to aya tha dctor*" she said "*abhi to leke ayi hoon*" again I ignored. Doctor said "*ye to bilkul theek hain inko to kuch nahi hua*". As I returned back hostel my classmates were there waiting for me and as I entered they stated, "*tera accident hua tha humne suna.. chal party de*".

As far as affair part is concerned, my family knew about Rishi, and I was permitted to meet him.

After the end of final year I came back to Lucknow and Rishi came to airport to meet my family and remained in Bangalore. All my family members came to take me back and now I had to decide further and this time my total percentage was 67.

As I came back to Lucknow my family took me to a priest to know my future and my family was shocked and disappointed to know that I will get married after 38 years but my family knew that Rishi is already in my life so it should not take that much time. That priest told me "*you might have raised like a normal girl but you are not normal, you were strong devotee of Shiva in past life*" I was like.. how does it matter for me.. I am same as all but as you all know things were actually happening strange with me for which I was not bothering.

Now, it was the time for my master's degree and after all the if and but we decided that I will shift to Dehradun for my M.Sc. Biotech. I was interviewed in Dolphin PG institute Dehradun for admission and I was happy to receive the admission letter from there. I had two options either to stay with Papa as he was posted there or I shift to hostel. I decided to shift to hostel to not miss my master's fun. My roommate was Pratibha, she was my classmate also and a good roommate. I could say that because we actually fought less.

One day in college lab everyone was discussing which guy look handsome to whom. At my turn I said R. Mehta, he was my senior, he was tall, dark, handsome to my eye but not to anyone else I feel. After that announcement strange things started happening with me. Sometime I see him in my class just to see me. One day he entered my class room looked at me and went. It started getting usual and one day in lunch hour he sung song with his classmates in dining area "*Is tarah Ashiqui ka asar chod jaunga*" but I had a feeling that only I am listening it and no one else and then my inner voice said "*this song will be remixed and you would love it*" (remix is available now and I love it). I didn't know what was happening so I decided to meet Mr. Mehta and tell him that I am already in a relationship. I went to him next day and took him a side and asked "*do you like me?*" he started laughing "*No, I have a girlfriend*". I was shocked, what was that? Again, I ignored as I didn't have any proof for anything. My inner voice said "*ye wo nahi hai*" I was like "*kaun wo?*"

It was the time of college feast now; all Dehradun was invited. Girls were excited to see guys from different college I remember I was in yellow suit and getting huge compliments from everyone. Suddenly, a guy appeared in front of my eyes as if he was of some different college, he was in tie and uniform. I wanted to see him more; he was looking at me only and in few seconds he vanished. This was time, I thought for the first time "*ye kya hota hai mere saath*" I wanted to see him again and was searching him everywhere but you can't win from God though he keeps showing his presence when you win God.

As we reach final year there was a guest lecturer came from Chandigarh to teach us about Intellectual property rights. It was a new subject for all of us and we all were curious about it. The lecture was for half an hr. but I listened it for 40 minutes, my dream broke when my classmate said "*tu kya dekh rahi hai aise*" I said "*wo padha raha na*" she said "*wo to chala gaya kab ka.. tu apni duniya me rehti hai*" and I saw lecturer smiling and leaving the class.

We all had reached the end now and final year dissertation was going on everyone was studying for Ph.D. exam. I did my dissertation from CDRI (Central Drug Research Institute) Lucknow one of the India's best drug institutes and I realized Ph.D. is not my cup of tea and as guided I planned for Intellectual property rights. My family was happy now with my results, I received 75.5% in M.Sc. Biotech. I was rising in every step unaware of the fact how far I could go.

# 4. First Job

After doing my Masters in Biotech I was quite frustrated because I want to work for a year before getting married and as Biotechnology, IPR (Intellectual property rights) was also very new filed. I was not getting job, was trying to compromise on different field, even cried. I didn't know where life was going as I had grown very ambitious but nothing rosy I had ever seen till date and then hell was still to pass.

Then papa really helped me a lot, he introduced me to a lecturer who was planning to start a company in IPR at Chandigarh and luckily, I got in. That was the company where I actually learnt the norms of IPR and other related aspects of it. I loved this field, something I like and love to do daily. Understanding invention, drafting application, filing patents, examination and grant, all used to give me another level of satisfaction.

Now, it was end of the year and I was in pressure to get married and I knew I had to resign as I would have to shift Noida after marriage. I got engaged in Chandigarh only and I kept this as secret in office so that they don't discriminate me in work but somehow, they got this news and hired a new employee. As the wedding day was coming near, I resigned but I would never forget that one year of experience in which I actually learned IPR which created my basic of the field.

# 5. The Marriage

I returned to Lucknow for the preparation of marriage. One day an *Aghori* came to our house, some priest told us that he helps people so was invited at home. I was curious to see so I alone went inside drawing room and was scared. Immediately, he said "*don't worry, I cannot harm you. I just came to see you*". He was worshiper of Goddess Durga. I started thinking why would he come to see me and my mom entered the room. We had discussion about marriage but I didn't find him more excited about it. He just said "*Shiv ji always keep an eye on you, please stay happy. If you be upset, he will also get upset.*" I was like ☹

For Horoscope matching we went to the same priest who told my marriage age as more than 38 and I was only 24 that time. He saw the *kundali* and said "*it is ok we can go ahead with marriage*" but he gave me different look as if he was saying "*don't marry, it's not the time*". I was little confused by his look but I ignored it.

Preparation was on boom and day by day the big day was coming around. Everybody was working to make the marriage smooth as much as one could control though still as all Indian wedding rituals were getting performed late. I was sitting in bridal attire in hotel room and my sister entered the room and had a very weird experience. She was in last year Diwali dress and crying "*please don't get married he is not the one, you won't be happy with him*" I was like "*what are you saying*" and she vanished and I forgot the incident. The bell rang and a short heighted beautiful guy entered the room with Paneer snacks, he said papa send him so that I can eat something. He served me that and again my sis came in her present-day attire, by that time I had finished my snacks and guy had gone. She said "*baraat aa gai, tumko bhook laga hoga na*" I said "*nahi abhi snacks khaye*" but tissue and container both was not present in the room. So, I decided not to elaborate more.

As I stepped out, for a second I got a view that marriage ground is empty but ground was full of people and relatives. Rishi and me were sitting on stage and my designer clip was coming out of my hair. My makeup artist said let me fix it and I don't know what happened to me I said to leave it and she said from the back "*let it be in second marriage you will look more beautiful*" I was shocked and looked back but she was not there. All functions performed on time and first time I saw my father and brother dancing so it was a kind of immense pleasure for me. After *jaimaal* we all went for *shaadi* ritual in *pandaal.* I noticed Dadaji (the aghori, I told earlier) witnessed whole marriage and was smiling all the time.

In the morning *shaadi* was done and I came to Noida for my new life.

After few months only I understood that we are highly incompatible and can't communicate with each other. One day I called papa to tell it's not happening but papa gave me a lecture of almost 45 mins that it's a new relationship and I should give time and he hang the phone. That was time of *Navratri* and I was talking to papa in front on Goddess Kaali. As I was about to go back home papa again called me and asked me what happened, I was out of my feet. I said papa "*abhi to baat hui thi 45 mins*" he said I just called u beta and papa too was shocked but he didn't give more importance and said just give some time.

After the span of one and a half year I got the job in corporate that to in IPR. Company is one of the leading IPR company in the world, very female friendly with good leaves count. I was so happy to join there.

One day I saw a guy in office taking lunch from dining area when I saw his face he vanished. This was the first time when I saw Shiva with brown eyes.

After my marriage I went several places out of India and everywhere Shiva showed his presence. The first was Hong Kong, Macao. It's a beautiful country and I witnessed him in a monastery. I saw him staring me and my husband was not able to notice that and as I saw him, he vanished.

Thailand was second, Rishi took me to buffet at a place in Phuket and he went washroom and my inner voice said " *ye tumhara pati nahi hai, wo baad me ayega*" I ignored as I took my food and coming back to my seat, I heard a father telling story to their children "*and the king and queen stayed happily ever after*" when I saw at the table there was only couple and as I moved forward, again I saw a very handsome God like human who took a bite in front of me and vanished and Rishi entered as I took my place. I had nothing to say again.

I thought now life is set but future had kept something more horrifying than anyone could think. I was a good employee and used to work really hard but hell came closer to me after I spent a time of 2 years in Clarivate. (earlier known as CPA Global). I started feeling that something is moving on my leg, started noticing balancing problem, was feeling my body in very unusual way, started listening few voices which was not real. I started fighting with my colleagues because I used to hear something they never said. Situation was getting worse day by day and everybody was complaining about me. I went to hospital to get whole body checked but everything was normal.

I don't know what was happening with me. I had to go to US first time that year. I went there with Rishi and mystical things were happening their also. Rishi was not able to make a call and I said give me I can do it. I took the phone and dialed the number and phone connected. My sister came to New York to meet me who was studying that time in Arizona State University and brought me a white dress with purple lipstick as I wore that dress my noticed sudden increase in my stomach area and I started looking weird. My sis said , you need to work on your figure. I couldn't explain what happened so I didn't say anything. We went to see world best IT University Massachusetts Institute of Technology (MIT). Me and my sister were roaming inside the university when I saw someone sitting and working on laptop. Damn, he was so hot I don't have words to explain. I saw him and he saw me for a second and as usual he disappeared from my eyes. This time I told my sis "*wahan koi baitha than na*" my sis was "*humko to koi nahi dikha*" I said " *bohot handsome tha*" she said " *yahan zyadatar log handsome hi hote hain*" now I had to stop because I knew she won't understand. We visited entire east coast of USA and came back and I witnessed Shiva at Statue of Liberty too at New York.

I was still not well. Now my colleagues were scared of me and no one wanted to talk to me which compelled me to put on papers. I still remember the pain and explained everything to mummy papa they thought I have some mental issues so they called me Lucknow and took me to a psychiatrist.

I went to the best doctor of Lucknow and after knowing all the symptoms he said I am suffering from "*Schizophrenia*". A kind of mental illness where a person stays in illusion and depart from actual life. But, was that actually happening to me? I couldn't ask this question that time but now I know it was not illness. I believe that I was just getting punished for my deeds. My weight was increasing through medicine I was losing confidence. Though I was recovering because it was mental medicine to work properly. Every night after dinner I used to have feeling that Shiva is taking walk with me with his *Trishul*. I said this to mummy and papa but they believed that it will go through medicine. But I had strange feeling of being a different girl.

We went to the same priest to tell that marriage is not working, I resigned from job and also about my illness. He said it's not any illness, you don't need medicine. He told me to worship Shiva and I said "*wo mere saath roz chlte hain uski kya pooja karun, dost hain mere mujhse baat karte hain*". Priest looked at me and said you don't know what are you saying even worshiper who do prayers for decades in mountains don't get such experiences what you are getting. But I said "*it's of no use, I lost everything*". He said "*later on you will know its importance. Actually, you don't need to take medicine"* but mummy interrupted *"then how will she recover?"* then he said *"ok take medicine"*.

There was a lot of to and fro between Lucknow and Noida in all this duration and one fine day I decided I will not go back. I was completely recovered long back and took this decision of my own. My parents supported and I started staying at Lucknow only.

# 6. Divorce and The Diamond Ring

It was 2017 when I came back to Lucknow and decided to never go back. I wanted to start working again but Lucknow was not a good place for jobs, as opportunities were really less that time. I worked in various fields like HR, business management though salary was very low.

It was 2019, when I was scrolling mobile content, I saw an ad of Mrs. India Worldwide 2019. They were calling for audition even in Lucknow. I thought to give it a try. It was in Hilton hotel Lucknow in Feb 2019 which was quite near to my home. I went there and was quite nervous but something magical happened before they called my name on stage. I got a feeling that "*all the judges who will judge my potential are humans*" and my nervousness wiped away. I rocked the stage with my dance, walk and answers. I came back home with a confidence that I am selected and I announced at home "*I will get selected*". After few days I got the confirmation email of selection.

On other side me and Rishi filed mutual divorce and the final call was in December.

I was selected as finalist for this beauty pageant and went Greece for finale in October 2019. This was the first feather on my cap. Though I was not the winner it was a good experience about life and expectations.

I have usually seen Shiva in white shirt and black pant. Here too he was there to see me with green eyes.

The day came when me and Rishi had to depart. We went to the court with two lawyers who were taking care of our case. We were waiting for our turn patiently when Rishi said "*you wait here, I am coming*" and he went out, as I moved around, I saw Rishi standing at the back with the help of wall and smiling. All of a sudden, he grew more handsome and before I could understand anything he disappeared. Rishi came inside and asked if the official called our names. I said "*no*". After sometime officials called our names and we got divorce mutually.

As I came back home, I noticed that one diamond from my engagement ring fallen out and my finger got a small cut. I write shayaris so that day I wrote these lines.

"Ek rishte ne yun jhatka ki zindagi palat gai meri,

Ek heera gira us anguthi se aur ungali kat gai meri"

# 7. The Mysteries

When I came back from Greece I decided to start my own company in intellectual property rights with the name of Valiant IP Support. It was tough though to start in Lucknow. Few people helped me in that. I was trying to bring all the IPR seekers, IPR providers, investors and idea holders on same platform as IPR is very important for new businesses. My plan was to create data pool. We created a dynamic website in January 2020 unaware of the fact that Corona was to ring the doorbell.

In March, April all my clients started dragging their hands back so I had to shut it down. Though I tried enough months to keep it running but it was of no use.

In June 2021, I again started a new content company where we were not only considering content but, we were trying to bring work in Tanglines, slogans, hashtags, customized poetries etc. Company was not sinking but I feel in UP people doesn't accept new things soon so it was tough for me to manage, again I shut it down.

Now it was a difficult time I didn't know what to do. I was looking guy for my second marriage too and no one was fitting my expectations. Same time again something mysterious started happening. I saw the song "dil na todunga" and I fell in love with the voice of the singer. I still don't know who sung that song. The music company says Abhi Dutt but I am sure someone else sung who don't want to disclose his name. I saw Siddharth Gupta for the first time. Then comes the remix of "Is tarah Ashiqi ka" Siddharth Gupta was looking very nice. That was the time when I found him most handsome man and supernaturally fallen in love with him. That was ultimate hell because it was never ending journey of illusion. I was taking medicine still I was able to feel his presence around me and in all of his songs including "*is tarah ashiqui ka*" I saw his eyes to be blue. No doubt, I still like his looks and I find him really handsome though I don't know why all handsome guys becomes actor 😊. Anyway.

Some of you could think that I might be going through black magic so I tell you, in black magic medicine doesn't work and it kills you. It was something else. I told in the beginning there was an evil and Shiva who protects me. This drama ended soon as Shiva saved me from hypnotism. One day I was looking into the blue eyed pic of Siddharth Gupta and all of a sudden, I felt a sudden hit on my head and everything normalized. You all can notice his eyes are brown in most of his songs not blue.

It was year 2022, I was confirmed that I am completely well so I stopped taking my medicine which was one small tablet on 0.5mg. For few days I remained good, felt well and excited but then again hell started I got very strong illusion that my family is not good for me. They don't love and care for me so I decided to run from my house. It was again a trauma for whole family as my father was already expired in 2019. In Feb 2022 I ran from my house to Bangalore. I planned everything but due to sim I was caught. My brother really harassed a lot due to all legal work. I was staying in a PG where mummy and *mausi* arrived and I insulted them and sent back. I couldn't imagine how my mom could have retuned back to Lucknow without taking me. I stayed in Bangalore for 6 months and it was all hell. I was not doing anything. Was in imaginary world, kept changing PG once my family come to know about it, finally they lost touch with me. If you will ask my experience, I used to sit in room for 10-15 days without eating anything. I saw that evil putting me in air and throwing me down on bed. I ate uncooked food because he told me we are going to different world. Shockingly my PG people was very normal with me as if they see me daily. My family knew my last PG where my mom used to come to see me without my information. I thought I will not survive now because I was out of the world, my body was in pain, more than labor pain. But, some power was there by which I was not dyeing. He told me, on 15$^{th}$ August you will go from this PG. I ran from house so I didn't had guts to call mom, they feel insulted in society because of me. But that divine power made me call my mom who was already in Bangalore and I called "*mummy please le chalo yahan se*". it was 15$^{th}$ August. My *chacha* was staying in Bangalore so we decided to go their first and evil was still there. In entire way to his house, he was compelling me to come with him. At his home also I was completely in his control. My cousin also came to see me. I felt as if evil is holding me in his arms and not letting me go anywhere. mummy was crying and me too. "*why me? What have I done? Why every time me? What is the conclusion of all this? What he wants?*". Though gradually he was losing grip. My family wanted me to take medicine and I wasn't taking so with the help of nurse they applied injection forcefully and admitted me to hospital. After treatment of 2 weeks, I came back to Lucknow. Entire 2023 went in recovering and in Nov 2023 was the last hit of my lifetime.

I was completely well again now and time was passing Diwali when I was praying Shiva as I do daily. That day when I opened my eyes, I felt tears on my cheeks though I wasn't crying. I asked shiva "*now what?*" This time I stayed at home only but completely cutoff from family. Evil inside my head stopped me again from taking medicine and I was fighting with my family daily and I told them I will search the guy with whom I will marry and professionally I was doing good. There was no one in my eye. I fooled my family till August 2024 when my mummy started giving medicine in my food and I realized my family is good. The evil always isolated me and tried to kill me. This time evil was successful to make me realize that I am a Goddess and I don't need to worship Shiva though I realized it soon and started praying. Shiva helped me when I shifted to different room, he compelled me to shift to the same room. Evil was trying to convince me that my future husband is Varun Thapar (he is a big industrialist, handsome and never married). Girls google it out 😊. I was out of my mind and send almost 200 messages on twitter to him but guess what Shiva was with me. Nothing got delivered. I wish someday he read my experiences and laugh 😊.

Conclusion is still to come keep reading.

# 8. Heart Break

By 2021 my profile grew well. I had 2 startups, was a beauty pageant finalist, had a state level position in CIMSME, published a book. Received various awards as entrepreneur and Author. Still, was not able to find Mr. right for my second marriage.

One priest told me to do a very tough worship of *Devi Katyayani*. He said if I do this worship continuously for 21 days and 5 hours daily, I will get to know who my husband is. "*It's very tough but if you will do it, you might meet your future husband even in middle of the pooja*". I took the oath to do it. I started in February 2021 and I met a guy on 15th February 2021 through Bumble. It was very sudden. We swiped right and next day we had coffee meet.

He was a handsome guy but he was using very tough English which was a turn off for me. I had to say "*Use simple English*". He told his name as A. Gupta who works in Google Gurgaon and currently working from home in Lucknow due to Corona.

He said he don't use social media because his father is in Anti-terrorist department at very high position and mom is a doctor in KGMC. *(bohot phek raha tha)*. We hardly sat for 30 mins and he had to go. I came back home and didn't like him in first impression. But I don't know why I wanted to meet him again. So, I pinged him again he said he can't come. He started making excuses when I ask for a meet and here *Katyayani mantras* was taking over me. I fell in love with him supernaturally and it was divine this time. I used to message everything to him so that he could understand it but he thought I am unwell and blocked me. I could not explain in worlds what is a divine love and how it feels like. But I had a question in my mind why I fell for him and not him? Then I thought because I explained everything, he might couldn't relate to it scientifically and blocked me. Earlier he was ok later on things got weird and he blocked me forever. I explained him everything because some power was driving me to do this. I thought that was an end as I can't explain the pain and intensity.

Later on, I came to know that no one should do these mantras of *Katyayani Devi* without the help or supervision of any priest. So, it became unnatural for me. Though I want to mention that it was not a human-like love. I still sense it sometime. (God -Goddess)

I am over it now and happy that he didn't accept me because I think he was a fake guy. I tried to find about him in Google through my friends but no one was like him. The person whom he mentioned as his father has different son. So, I have moved on.

Search was still going and I decided to join gym near my house to Anytime Fitness, Gomti Negar Lucknow. Hell was again waiting for me inside. I saw a guy in gym same like A. Gupta but short heighted. My mind was getting engaged in all unnatural thigs in gym. I used to see what was not in gym A. Gupta was one of it. Evil again played with my mind and made me believe that short A. Gupta (same as of my height) is in love with me. I lost my mind when one day evil in my mind said he is waiting for me in gym and when I went, I couldn't see anyone inside. I thought this time I will not survive as I was turning mad but again in washroom, I got a sudden jerk and became completely normal. I love you Shiva for every protection. I don't like A. Gupta anymore but that unnatural feeling still haunts me sometime.

# 9. Past Life Regression

Past Life regression or (PLR) is a process that uses meditation or Hypnotism to help people access their memories from previous lives. I know in this era of AI maximum people don't believe in PLR or reincarnation but I have gone through it.

I was little disturbed because I was not able to find a guy for marriage in these many years and the major issue was none of them attracted me enough to meet again after one coffee meet. I decided I will try to find the answer through PLR.

The day came and instructor said it will take a total of one and a half hours. I have gone through this process few days back only. Instructor took me to a deep meditation and awaken my soul to travel in the past. After completing verbal meditation suddenly, he asked "*look at the sky what do you see*" I saw it was written 1856 then he asked where am I. I was in Madhopur (MP) (place still exists). He said to look down and I saw my feet I was wearing *khadau* (wooden slipper). I was wearing saffron cloths with *rudraksh* garland in my neck and had a *kamandal* in my hand. He asked me "*what do you do?*" I said "*I am worshiper of Shiva*". I saw myself in a market where no one was scared of me but I was very arrogant because of my powers I achieved due to devotion.

I saw I used to stay alone with a girl and pursued death in young age though euthanasia (*Iccha mrityu*). I was a very strong devotee of shiva I saw the way I used to do *pooja*. (I don't do even 1% of that in this life time though I do worship daily) Still my purpose was not solved. Why am I not getting attracted to any guy?

Instructor said try to find "*did you ever got married in any life time*". I saw my *swayamver* this time. I was a princess and I saw a prince in arena who was ugly. It made me insult him though he was very brainy. He was completely heartbroken and left that place. Instructor asked to apologies him so I try to do it but he was not forgiving me. I again said sorry through my heart, this time he said OK but he said he will meet me in this life time. I don't know the time though.

Instructor said you were devotee of shiva let me try if you can see future. He asked me "*how's world in 3024?*". I was able to see a world where there is an equality between robots and humans. Robots could not reproduce but have seen humans working for robots in home as well as office and same was with humans; robots were working at home as well as office.

He again asked "*can you see people believe in God after 50K years or not?*". I was able to see clearly that I had a big temple at home and I was worshiping shiva. Now, he started to bring me back and I came back in few seconds. It was an ultimate experience and I got my answer. Instructor seems happier than me. He told me "*It's not easy to take people in past life many can't do it but I am really happy that you were a worshiper which made easy for me to do my work*".

# 10. My Beliefs

I was going through unnatural incidents since childhood though I never gave importance to it. As I grew up, I suffered a lot in every aspect of life. I believe being devotee of Shiva I always asked him only a husband like him. As per the priest I had to get married after 38 but you can't change destiny. Now I am divorced and was not able to get attracted towards any guy reason you all know. But I am born special due to my devotion to Shiva so he protected me from the Evil who was stopping to meet my desire and Shiva protected me every time and saved me to reach him. The one he has selected for me.

# 11. The Wait

I have seen all colors of love till date. I was able to recall incidents because Shiva is more prominent with me now a days. He is guiding me to write this book. I sense his presence almost every day and medicine are continued.

Few days back in the morning I was listening to a romantic song and A. Gupta again started haunting me, that time I felt that Shiva is holding my hand on my bed and I wished him to play some Shiva song in my headphone and you won't believe all Shiva songs started playing in my headphone, that too skipping the one I am not very fond off.

Yesterday 19th November 2024 I got a request from a guy on a matrimony site and I ignored it. I already saw his profile which he keeps deleting. It was morning and music stopped in my headphone as if I had to accept his request. I accepted it and asked the reason of frequent removal of his profile. He said "*my parents don't know how to use app properly so he had to delete because of mistakes*" and heard a voice within "*he could be a prospect*" and music started.

I know I am special and someone is made for me. Shiva is helping me to reach him by showing his presence.

**"main dar nahi rahi, mujhe pata hai tum aoge. I am waiting"**

# My Wisdom Through My Connection with Lord Shiva

Shiva is more about love than destruction. He owned 3$^{rd}$ eye because he is most powerful due to his infinite love.

Ganga can't flow from Shiva's head. He is one woman man so he cannot accept any other woman in any part of his body. I don't believe in this concept.

When Goddess Kaali was destroying universe in anger Shiva lie down in front of her, not to protect Universe but to decrease Goddess Kaali anger. He could have stopped the destruction by himself as both are equally powerful but he didn't want to hurt her by doing something against her wish. So, he took another way. He is the most loving husband.

River Narmada decided never to get married when she was betrayed by her childhood love and started flowing in opposite direction. Every stone of river Narmada is a Shivling. It was Narmada pure love which compelled Shiva to change every stone of the river to a Shivling.

"Where there is a pure love there is Shiva"